OSLO
THE CITY AT A GL...

Aker Brygge
Regeneration of this 185... in 1985, and it boasts bui... Økaw, Niels Torp and Kari... Development is ongoing; ... of the Nobel Peace Center (see p036).

Uranienborg church
Norwegian architect Balthazar Conrad Lange's 1886 brick design was renovated by Arnstein Arneberg in 1930 in a Gothic-revival style, with stained-glass windows by Emanuel Vigeland.
Uranienborgveien 22b, T 2362 9080

Royal Palace
This neoclassical pile was designed by Danish-born Hans Ditlev Frantz Linstow and finished in 1849. It was renovated under current King Harald V and is open to the public in summer.
Henrik Ibsens gate 1, T 2204 8700

Holmenkollen ski jump
The capital's most iconic structure opened in 1892, and was a venue for the 1952 Winter Olympics. It is being rebuilt by Copenhagen-based architects JDS and will reopen in 2011.
Kongeveien 5, T 2292 3200

Operahuset
The new opera house underpins the gradual transformation of the entire Oslo waterfront.
See p010

St Hanshaugen park
There are great city views from this charming park that is a hive of activity all year round.

Peace Research Institute Oslo
This influential body was founded in 1959. Since 2005 it has been housed in a former gasworks, sparking local gentrification.
Hausmanns gate 7, T 2254 7700

INTRODUCTION
THE CHANGING FACE OF THE URBAN SCENE

Oslo has been dubbed the Blue-Green City as it lies between a fjord and a national park. It looks especially pretty in the wonderfully iridescent summer sunlight or from the window of a candelit café when the streets are blanketed by snow. Oslo is low density and small, and the fact that there has never been any coherent city planning seems to sum up the pervading laid-back attitude.

Oslo-ites are highly educated, open and friendly, and live life at a gentle pace. With one of the youngest populations in Europe, the city's bars and restaurants are thriving, and each of its many self-contained neighbourhoods has a unique character, making Oslo a joy to wander around and discover for yourself. The cultural calendar is littered with festivals and events, though the city does turn eerily quiet in July and August, when its residents retreat en masse to their home towns or summer cabins. Some venues close, but it is still an excellent time to explore the city.

The Norwegian tendency towards self-deprecation often leads locals to ask why anyone would want to visit this 'little village of ours on the outskirts of the world', but such a question is easily answered. Oslo is fast developing a burgeoning pool of world-class creative talent – not least architects Snøhetta, film director Joachim Trier and fashion designers Batlak og Selvig – all of whom have slowly been reinventing the cultural landscape and establishing Oslo as a must-visit Scandinavian destination.

ESSENTIAL INFO
FACTS, FIGURES AND USEFUL ADDRESSES

TOURIST OFFICE
Jernbanetorget 1
T 8153 0555
visitoslo.com

TRANSPORT
Car hire
Avis
Munkedamsveien 27
T 8156 9044
avis.com
Public transport
T-bane (metro)
T 2208 4240
www.tbane.no
Taxis
Norgestaxi
T 08 000
Oslo Taxi
T 02 323

EMERGENCY SERVICES
Ambulance
T 113
Fire
T 110
Police
T 112
24-hour pharmacy
Jernbanetorgets Apotek
Jernbanetorget 4b
T 2241 2482

EMBASSIES
British Embassy
Thomas Heftyes gate 8
T 2313 2700
www.britain.no
US Embassy
Henrik Ibsens gate 48
T 2244 8550
norway.usembassy.gov

MONEY
American Express
DnB NOR bank
Stranden 1, Aker Brygge
T 9150 4800
travel.americanexpress.com

POSTAL SERVICES
Post Office
Jernbanetorget 1
T 8100 0710
Shipping
UPS
Ulvenveien 75b
T 8003 3470

BOOKS
Norway: A Guide to Recent Architecture
by Ingerid Helsing Almaas (BT Batsford)
Oslo 1960-1980 by Jon Gunnar Arntzen
and Stig-Audun Hansen (Kom Forlag)

WEBSITES
Art/Architecture
afmuseet.no
doga.no
nasjonalmuseet.no
Newspaper
norwaypost.no

COST OF LIVING
**Taxi from Gardermoen Airport
to city centre**
£70
Cappuccino
£3
Packet of cigarettes
£8.20
Daily newspaper
£2.50
Bottle of champagne
£65

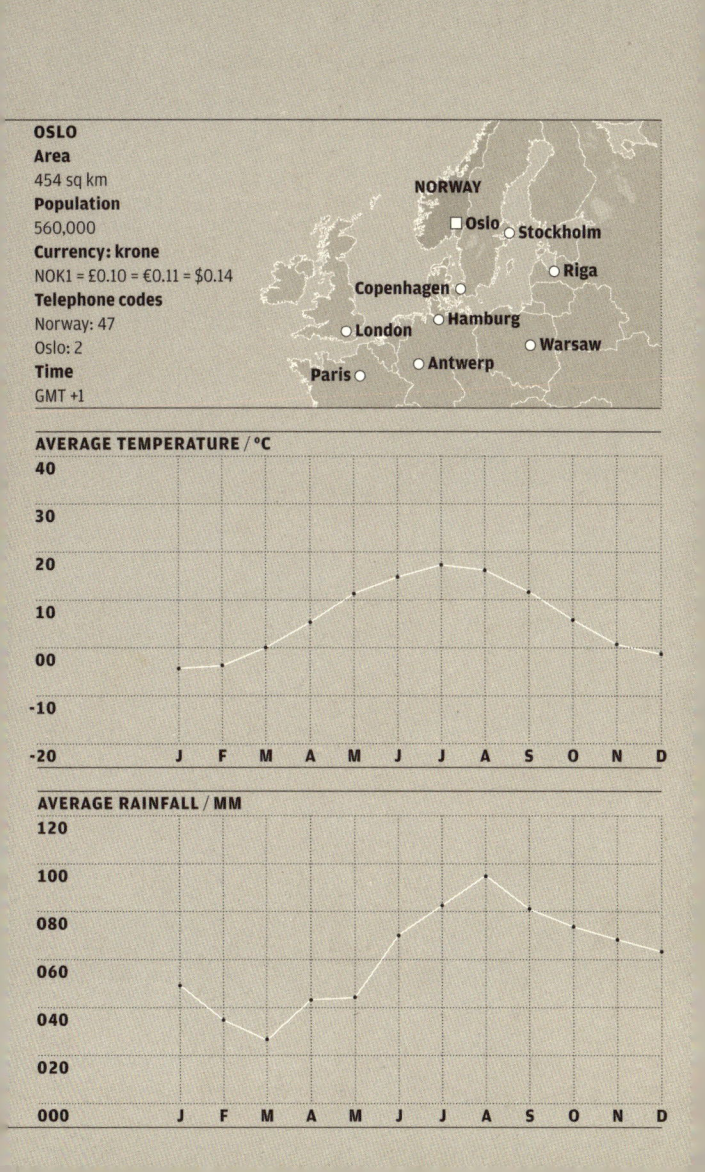

OSLO
Area
454 sq km
Population
560,000
Currency: krone
NOK1 = £0.10 = €0.11 = $0.14
Telephone codes
Norway: 47
Oslo: 2
Time
GMT +1

AVERAGE TEMPERATURE / °C

AVERAGE RAINFALL / MM

NEIGHBOURHOODS
THE AREAS YOU NEED TO KNOW AND WHY

To help you navigate the city, we've chosen the most interesting districts (see below and the map inside the back cover) and colour-coded our featured venues, according to their location; those venues that are outside these areas are not coloured.

FROGNER
Cobbled streets of neoclassical apartments are where Oslo's old money lives, while quality bistros, galleries and independent furniture shops nestle among embassies on picturesque side roads. Frognerparken boasts the Vigeland Sculpture Park (see p013) as well as a wonderful lido.

MAJORSTUEN
A mix of smart residential properties set around Oslo's most upmarket retail street, this area has a cosmopolitan air, with high-end international labels and homegrown designers such as Iselin Engan. Preppy locals hang out north of the T-bane, where you'll find Colosseum Kino (see p069) and the pan-Asian eaterie Nodee (see p050).

GRÜNERLØKKA
During the last decade, renovated lofts, delis and boutiques, such as Sjarm (see p074), have given this former working-class area a new lease of life. It is full of bars, clubs and gig venues, often with cutting-edge design, and guerrilla stores selling anything from skateboards to shoes.

VIKA
The business district is the focal point for Oslo's weekend partying – La Belle Sole (see p060) is the pick of the clubs. Brush yourself off in the morning for brunch at Pascal Café de la Paix (see p041) and visit the Ibsen Museum (Henrik Ibsens gate 26, T 2212 3550) for something highbrow.

URANIENBORG AND BRISKEBY
This charming residential area has a mix of architectural styles, from art nouveau to postmodern. Take a walk from Uranienborg church (Uranienborgveien 22b, T 2362 9080) along the tree-lined Gyldenløves gate. Dotted around are neighbourhood cafés and antiques shops.

BISLETT AND ST HANSHAUGEN
Young professionals starting families are attracted by this area's gentle pace and well-kept, high-ceilinged apartments set in blocks with communal courtyards. There's a mix of unselfconscious cafés and easygoing bars, and St Hanshaugen park is a popular green space. Also worth a visit is the Gamle Aker church (see p012).

SENTRUM
The main shopping district has the usual department stores and chains. However, to the south of Karl Johans gate, Oslo's medieval heritage can be seen in buildings such as the Akershus Castle (see p009). The area also now boasts interesting boutiques like Freudian Kicks (see p086).

GRØNLAND
Priced out of Grünerløkka, students and creative types have moved into Grønland, home since the 1970s to Pakistani migrants and latterly Somalis and Kurds. High-density social housing sits cheek-by-jowl with trendy new-builds. The most dynamic part of Oslo, it's definitely in the ascendant.

LANDMARKS
THE SHAPE OF THE CITY SKYLINE

Huge oil reserves were discovered on the continental shelf in the 1970s, but it is only now that Oslo's traditionally conservative city fathers are starting to green-light ambitious public projects that are a feature of other Scandinavian capitals. A clutch of statement buildings will arrive in the coming years as the former docklands undergoes a regeneration known as Fjord City (see p064), which began with the 2008 inauguration of the Operahuset (overleaf).

Oslo was founded in the Middle Ages, in Gamlebyen. Its oldest structure, Gamle Aker church (see p012), dates from 1150 and sits on an old silver mine, while the prominent Akershus Castle (Akershus festning, T 2309 3553) was commissioned by King Håkon V in 1299. Other useful orientation points in this low-rise city include Sentrum's late modernist 1975 Postgirobygget (Biskop Gunnerus gate 14) by architects Pedersen and Krognes and the 1990 Radisson SAS Plaza Hotel (Sonja Henies plass 3), Oslo's tallest building at 117m, by Swedish firm White Arkitekter. The Holmenkollen ski jump (Kongeveien 5, T 2292 3200) and the Nobel Peace Center (see p036) are icons of a more symbolic nature. By the same token, Gustav Vigeland's Sculpture Park (see p013) is a must-see on any agenda, but it his lesser-known brother's work, which is exhibited at the Emanuel Vigeland Museum (Grimelundsveien 8, T 2214 5788), that is considered by locals to be the city's hidden treasure. *For full addresses, see Resources.*

Operahuset
The glass-and-marble showpiece of the city's rebirth by architects Snøhetta rises glacier-like out of the Oslofjord. Its external ramps slope out of the water and up to the roof, symbolically reconnecting Oslo with the sea. Inside, the partially submerged, oak-lined auditorium has world-class acoustics.
Kirsten Flagstads plass 1, T 2142 2100, www.operaen.no

011 LANDMARKS

Gamle Aker church

This medieval limestone church dates back to the Viking era. The Roman-style basilica is impressive in its simplicity, although it has been damaged by fire several times, later alterations including the 1715 pulpit and 1861 tower. The church is still used by the local Lutheran parish and often hosts concerts while its peaceful grounds offer sanctuary from the hustle and bustle of nearby St Hanshaugen. Stroll down Akersveien afterwards to admire the conservation area's early-19th-century clapboard houses, painted vivid shades of blood red, royal blue and canary yellow, many of which now house artisan shops.
Akersbakken 26, T 2362 9120, gamle-aker.no

Vigeland Sculpture Park

Mandal-born Gustav Vigeland's magnum opus was a gift to his adopted home of Oslo. Mainly built between 1939 and 1949 and set within the rambling Frognerparken, this 32-hectare section is an immaculately manicured garden adorned with 212 bronze and granite sculptures. Influenced by ancient and renaissance themes, and the craftsmanship of peers such as Rodin, Vigeland's distinctly lifelike figures have an impressive physicality, and successfully celebrate the spectrum of human emotion. Effectively a world-class art exhibition on permanent outdoor display, Vigeland's legacy is an ambitious masterclass in scale, perspective and artistic endeavour.
Frognerparken

014

LANDMARKS

Nationaltheatret

This imposing neoclassical theatre, designed by architect Henrik Bull, sits in the heart of the city and had its grand opening in 1899. Following Norway's independence from Sweden in 1905, it became the symbolic focus of a new-found national pride, and the repertoire still makes the most of the theatre's strong association with Norway's most celebrated playwright, Henrik Ibsen, one of the fathers of modern drama. With rare exceptions, performances of classics such as *The Wild Duck* and *Lady From the Sea* are in the native language. However, you can take a guided tour of the theatre in English to admire its Norwegian-style Jugendstil interiors and 740-seat domed main hall in all its opulent turn-of-the-century splendour.
Johanne Dybwads plass 1, T 2200 1400, nationaltheatret.no

HOTELS
WHERE TO STAY AND WHICH ROOMS TO BOOK

Though Oslo doesn't lack decent hotels, it is found wanting when it comes to the type of stylish bolt-holes you expect in Scandinavia. Most are geared towards the business traveller, with the majority owned by chains, although there are a few exceptions. The Hotel Bastion (see p022) was a labour of love for businessman Morten Mørch, who filled it with prints and antique furniture with the help of designer Anamone W Våge, a legacy that has remained since it was taken over. The independent Lysebu (see p028) is run by the Fund for Danish-Norwegian Cooperation, and exudes understated chic.

For shopaholics, the Thon Hotel Gyldenløve (Bogstadveien 20, T 2333 2300) is well placed on this upmarket street, a haunt of label-hungry yummy-mummies. The hotel is more like a cool B&B, although its features, such as flat-screen TVs and chairs by Quinze & Milan, exceed much of what's on offer elsewhere. The Grims Grenka (opposite) was formerly the nondescript Hotel Nobel House, but since its transformation in 2008 is anything but grim, suggesting there is hope for boutique hotels with a design focus in Oslo. Hotly anticipated is the autumn 2009 opening of the 158-room Hotel Folketeateret (Storgata 21-13, T 2109 6500), part of a wider project by Eiendomsspar and Mellbye Arkitekter to renovate the 1935 Folketeater, designed by Morgenstierne and Arne Eide in 1926, and restore it to its original art deco glory.
For full addresses and room rates, see Resources.

Grims Grenka

Oslo's first design hotel didn't arrive until 2008, but it was worth the wait. Norwegian architect Kristin Jarmund's innovative design creates a cocoon-like ambience from the moment you enter the stylish lobby (overleaf). The pared-down Nordic aesthetic is coupled with Far Eastern influences in the 42 rooms – choose between summer and winter themes (202, 409, 414 are among the best) – while the 24 suites, such as the Loft Suite 410 (above), boast dark oak, shagpile rugs, freestanding baths and views of Akershus Castle (see p009). The rooftop Q Lounge has been adopted by Oslo's party crowd as *the* place to start the evening, while Madu, the Hakkasan-influenced restaurant, is a great venue for late-night cocktails.
Kongens gate 5, T 2310 7200,
www.grimsgrenka.no

Lobby, Grims Grenka

HOTELS

Hotel Gabelshus

Located in the residential neighbourhood of Skillebekk, yet just 10 minutes by tram from Sentrum, this charming hotel offers guests the opportunity to enjoy the city the way a local might. Behind its ivy-clad frontage are the austere interiors of a former townhouse, parts of which date from 1912. It merged with an adjoining hotel many years ago and was modernised in 2000. Public areas, such as the dining room (above), are furnished with a melange of stylish chairs and sofas that invite loitering. Ask for Suite 501 (right), up in the eaves, or Rooms 202, 210 and 311, which come with luxurious bathrooms and French balconies with views of the neighbouring embassies and well-appointed apartment blocks. Dinner at nearby Hos Thea (see p053) is highly recommended.
Gabels gate 16, T 2327 6500, gabelshus.no

HOTELS

Hotel Bastion
Located near Oslo's tiny red-light district, now home to hip watering holes and boutiques, the Bastion resembles the home of a 1920s big-game hunter, with its oak panels, battered Chesterfields and double-fronted antique chests. None of its 99 rooms are the same; we recommend Deluxe Room 316 (pictured).
Skippergaten 7, T 2247 7700, hotelbastion.no

HOTELS

Thon Panorama
Initially envisaged as a residential development but converted into a 118-room hotel by the time of completion, this no-frills option offers excellent service and a great location in the Kvadraturen, the historic quarter where Christian IV founded Christiania after the fire in 1624 (the city was renamed Oslo in 1925). Some of the rooms are a touch poky but offer value and have a clean design – wooden floors and simple, functional furniture. The 80 apartment-style rooms have working kitchens, although cutlery is only provided for long stays. Ask for Room 1104, 1109 or 1202, which come with a terrace, or one of the two penthouses – 1301 (above) overlooks the Operahuset (see p010) while 1302 (right) has a view towards Holmenkollen – both of which sleep up to six people.
Rådhusgata 7b, T 2331 0800, www.thonhotels.com/oslopanorama

HOTELS

Grand Hotel
In business since 1874, this hotel boasts a sweeping marble lobby complete with ornate mirrors. The playful Ladies Floor has 13 rooms inspired by Norwegian women, such as Sami musician Mari Boine (Arctic Room 575; pictured), while the Ibsen Suite 654 is popular with both Nobel winners and hip hop dignitaries.
Karl Johans gate 31, T 2321 2000, grand.no

HOTELS

Lysebu
Set in the grounds of a former farm 25 minutes outside Oslo, Lysebu comprises several adjoining lodges dating from 1916, and its unassuming exterior belies a wonderfully luxurious hotel. Rooms are pared back, with design classics such as 'Louis Ghost' chairs by Philippe Starck coupled with bespoke oak-framed beds, high-thread-count linen and horsebox-sized showers, as in Room 432 (above), and public areas boast vaulted barn-style ceilings and large, toasty fireplaces. Lysebu also has a fine in-house restaurant and one of the most highly regarded wine cellars in Norway, with no less than seven sommeliers. The hotel overlooks the beautiful Sørkedalen Valley, and beyond it, Nordmarka Forest (see p088).
*Lysebuveien 12, Holmenkollen,
T 2151 1000, www.lysebu.com*

Hotel Continental

A preppy feel pervades this handsome hotel designed by architect Ivar Cock in 1900. Many of its 155 rooms and the lobby (above) underwent extensive renovation in 2006 and 2007. They kept the hardwood parquet flooring, leather headboards, classic period furniture, vintage mirrors and neutral shades, but added some contemporary furniture. The hotel remains family-run, now into the fourth generation, which explains its reputation for faultless service. We recommend the Deluxe Room 507 (overleaf), while 729 has great views of the Nationaltheatret (see p014). The classy downstairs Theatercaféen (see p046) is a destination in its own right. *Stortingsgaten 24-26, T 2282 4000, hotel-continental.com*

Deluxe Room 507, Hotel Continental

HOTELS

24 HOURS
SEE THE BEST OF THE CITY IN JUST ONE DAY

Oslo is well served by an integrated network of trams, ferries, buses and an efficient metro, which makes it infinitely manageable. Start your day at the Frogner plass branch of United Bakeries (opposite); the entrance to Vigeland Sculpture Park (see p013) is just 20m away. Then wander down either Frognerveien or Bygdøy allé, both of which have a host of smart galleries and interiors shops, to Solli plass. From there you can jump on a tram or bus towards Sentrum to visit the National Museum of Architecture (overleaf), which shares the beautiful Bankplassen square with the Museum of Contemporary Art (Bankplassen 4, T 2198 2000), housed in the impressive Jugendstil-inspired former Norges Bank building. Walk back through the old quarter, home to many fashion boutiques, for lunch at the venerable Grand Café (see p035).

In the afternoon, head to Aker Brygge to visit the Nobel Peace Center (see p036) or take a tram east to the Norwegian Centre for Design and Architecture (DogA) (Hausmanns gate 16, T 2329 2870), located in a former power station converted by Oslo architects Jensen & Skodvin. We recommend Südøst (see p037) for dinner, before returning to Sentrum for cocktails at Posthallen (see p038) or, in summer, the rooftop terrace at Q Lounge (see p017). End the night dancing at the flashy Barbeint (Henrik Ibsens gate 60a, T 9506 4686) or the more grown-up La Belle Sole (see p060).
For full addresses, see Resources.

09.00 United Bakeries
This chic tea room is so popular with the neighbourhood's posh *barnevogn* (pushchair) mafia, you'll need hawk-like skills to land a table, especially in the courtyard on a sunny day. However, it is impressive how well behaved two-year-old Norwegians are – perhaps it's the promise of the chocolate flowing through the fountain in the window that can be ladled onto your order on request.

Inside, the whitewashed palette, reproduction 19th-century wallpaper, shabby-chic furniture, vintage lighting and rustic-style crockery add a touch of class to your morning hot chocolate and pastries. If you fancy trying a traditional Norwegian treat, then ask for one of the delicious *boller* (cinnamon buns).
Frognerveien 58, T 2411 8728, unitedbakeries.com

11.30 Museum of Architecture
Reopened in 2008 in this new location after a three-year hiatus, the National Museum of Architecture's permanent collection consists of original sketches, models, photographs and 3D visualisations charting the evolution of the country's built heritage, and introduces the work of up-and-coming architects. The building was designed by Christian Heinrich Grosch and opened in 1830 but had lain derelict since 1990. The redesign and extension was carried out by Pritzker Prize winner Sverre Fehn, who died in early 2009. The concrete exhibition pavilion has a green-blue glass façade, and is named after Jens Ulltveit-Moe, the industrialist whose £3.75m donation secured the project's go-ahead.
Bankplassen 3, T 2198 2100, nationalmuseum.no

13.00 Grand Café
This establishment opened in 1874 and has been a popular haunt for generations of intellectuals and artists. Its most famous patron, Henrik Ibsen, maintained a regular table (number 17) for twice-daily visits, a habit he picked up while in self-imposed exile in southern Europe. Indeed, the opulent style of the restored interior, with its dark oak panelling, high-backed leather banquettes and antique lighting, is reminiscent of the grand Renaissance-era Venetian and Florentine cafés. Covering the back wall is a mural by Per Krogh, which was installed in 1932 and depicts the café and its notable patrons in a scene from 1879. During the week the Grand is popular with businessmen, while weekends draw a broader crowd, thanks to one the best brunches in town.
Karl Johans gate 31, T 2321 2018, grand.no

15.30 Nobel Peace Center
Opened by King Harald V in 2005, this cutting-edge museum-cum-gallery concept by British architect David Adjaye, in collaboration with American designer David Small, exceeds expectations. It is housed in Oslo's handsome former Vestbanen railway station, which was built in 1872 and is now listed. Bold mood-enhancing colours fill an open-plan ground-floor space that hosts innovative exhibitions, and the first floor houses an array of high-tech interactive installations, such as the neon-lit 'garden' of fibreoptics topped with LCD screens ('Nobel Field'; above), each explaining the life and legacy of a former Nobel Laureate. Even the in-house Pascal Café de la Paix (see p041) has a jaw-dropping interior.
Rådhusplassen, T 4830 1000, www.nobelpeacecenter.org

19.30 Südøst
Perched beside an arched stone bridge on the Akerselva river, this art nouveau building served as a bank from WWI to the 1940s. Opened as a restaurant in 2005, it is fashionable yet unpretentious and perfectly encapsulates the mood of this hip neighbourhood, drawing a good-looking crowd of locals, art students and party-goers who hit the bars along Thorvald Meyers gate afterwards. Its high-ceilinged dining hall has an industrial feel with oversized windows, exposed brickwork and large fireplaces, while the long, open-plan kitchen turns out bistro-style classics. The wine cellar is housed in the former vaults.
Trondheimsveien 5, T 2335 3070, sydost.no

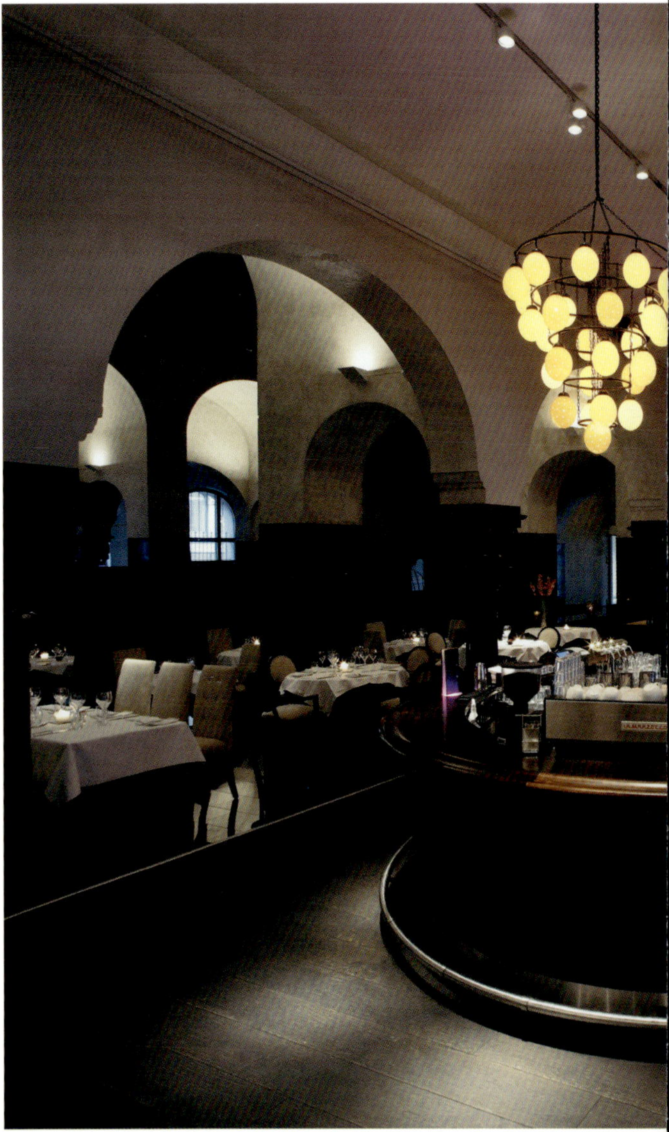

21.00 Posthallen
This early 20th-century neoclassical building was renovated into a bar/restaurant/café in 2008. Formerly the sorting office of the Norwegian postal service, it boasts triple-height ceilings supported by 11m marble columns. Its focal point is a leather-panelled island bar, lit by ostrich-eggshell chandeliers. *Prinsens gate 8, T 2241 1730, posthallenrestaurant.no*

URBAN LIFE
CAFÉS, RESTAURANTS, BARS AND NIGHTCLUBS

There is no getting away from the fact that Oslo is expensive, but you can take comfort in knowing the kitchen and waiting staff are better looked after here than in most of Europe's major capitals.

Aside from a few places that have a reputation for being midday destinations, such as Bølgen & Moi (see p051) or Grand Café (see p035), many restaurants don't open for lunch. Food-wise, there has been a move towards using traditional ingredients, prepared with classic French techniques, now often with Mediterranean and Asian influences; Norwegians are finding new ways to enjoy salmon, king crab, lobster and venison. Try Kampen Bistro (Bøgata 21, T 2219 7708), a kooky eaterie that is popular with the hipster crowd, or the Michelin-starred Restaurant Oscarsgate (Inngang Pilestredet 63, T 2246 5906), where the modest room (only 22 covers) does little to prepare you for Bjorn Svensson's imaginative cuisine.

For drinks, Oslo Mekaniske Verksted (Tøyenbekken 34, T 4523 7534) has a seriously cool vibe; fringe theatre fans should take the opportunity to pop next door to Det Åpne Teater (Tøyenbekken 34, T 2205 2800). The city's club scene is confined to a handful of super-charged venues, including The Villa (Møllergata 23), though many locals tend to prefer bars that put on gigs, such as Internasjonalen (see p059), Blå (Brenneriveien 9c, T 4000 4277) and Dattera til Hagen (Grønland 10, T 2217 1861).
For full addresses, see Resources.

Pascal Café de la Paix
Oslo's sweet-toothed citizens have enjoyed a love affair with French-born Pascal Dupuy's eponymous boutique café/pâtisseries since he opened his first at Tollbugata 11 (T 2242 1119) in 1995. There are now several dotted across town, each with an individual character. The most visually striking is Café de la Paix at the Nobel Peace Center (see p036). Its 'Earth Major Minor in Yellow and Green' mural by British artist Chris Ofili, which resembles asymmetrical shards of coloured glass, plays with perspective and makes the cavernous space feel more intimate. The accomplished kitchen serves bistro classics with recherché flourishes, such as creamy fish and saffron soup with salmon balls and prawns, and pickled cod on rye bread with goat's cheese and carrot cream.
Rådhusplassen, T 2283 0400, pascal.no

SW20

Double-height ceilings with restored oak panelling, marble floors and leather banquettes provide a sleek setting for SW20's elegantly turned-out English comfort food served with a French accent, which includes oxtail soup with poached egg, and lamb shank with potato purée. The name refers to the Wimbledon postcode where owner Dominic Gorham grew up, and the London connection is reinforced with a large 1960s photographic print of Michael Caine on an end wall. Having arrived in Oslo by way of several years in Paris working with the likes of Mourad Mazouz, Gorham established the restaurant in 2008 and runs it with a casual charm that has won locals over. It's only open in the evenings from Tuesday to Saturday.
Solligata 2, T 2255 0060, sw20.no

Åpent Bakeri Plaza
This renowned bakery employs traditional techniques to produce arguably the finest loaves in town. Opened in 2003, the branch in Ullevål Hageby is housed in a pavilion with an imposing façade that takes pride of place in a picturesque square. The premises have been in use as a bakery since 1929 and the artisan breads (almost exclusively wholemeal with all manner of grains, oats and rye) are made daily. Grab a croissant or *skolebolle* (Norwegian wheat bun with a cream and shredded coconut topping) to go, as you're unlikely to get a table. Then take a walk around the Harlad Hans-planned, Oscar Hoff-designed neighbourhood that began as a municipal housing project in 1916 but is now one of the most desirable enclaves in Oslo.
Damplassen 24-25, T 2204 9667, apentbakeri.no

Lofoten Fiskerestaurant

This place stands head and shoulders above most of the other restaurants and bars that currently fill the Aker Brygge complex. Opened in 1993, it was taken over in 1997 by head chef Bjørn Tore Furset, who retained the original stripped-back monochrome interior designed by Thomas Næss. With floor-to-ceiling windows looking out over the Oslofjord, the light-filled dining room is particularly busy around midday with power-lunchers. The simple fish and seafood dishes on offer are exceptional, while knowledgeable staff will explain the provenance of the day's catch. The restaurant is named after the north-west coastal fishing town famous for its *skrei* (Arctic cod), which is naturally on the menu when it's in season.
Stranden 75, T 2283 0808,
www.lofoten-fiskerestaurant.no

Olympen Mat & Vinhus
This used to be a genuine old-style 'brown' pub – a spit-and-sawdust relic from the days when the area was staunchly working class. Based on the concept of a German beer hall, cheap meals were served alongside an evening drink. Much of the neo-baroque dining room is protected and the period paintings date from 1928. In 2007 the owners gave it a hip makeover that is best described as rough glamour, adding glass chandeliers, bronze-framed mirrors and church-like pews. Unpretentious staff serve a no-nonsense gastro-pub menu, for example braised pork with sausage and pickled cabbage. Known as 'Lompa' to regulars, it is the embodiment of the new east Oslo scene.
Grønlandsleiret 15, T 2410 1999, olympen.no

Theatercaféen
Part of Hotel Continental (see p029), this dining hall opened in 1900 and is one of the most elegant in Oslo. The parquet flooring, vaulted stucco ceiling, intricate woodwork and marble columns were all painstakingly restored in 1971 following a botched modernisation in 1949. The food is standard all-day brasserie fare. *Stortingsgaten 24-26, T 2282 4000, theatercafeen.no*

URBAN LIFE

Mauds

Head chef Brede Bystadhaugen took over from his mother in 1997 and moved Mauds to its current location in 2005. The menu remains characteristic of the solid, honest flavours that define Norwegian cuisine, which are now being rediscovered by cosmopolitan Oslo-ites. Timeless dishes include fillet of marinated herring with onion, sour cream, pickled beetroot and potatoes, and braised shank of reindeer served with dried mushroom cream sauce, roast vegetables and potato purée. The atmospheric 1920s-style dining room combines frayed vintage rugs, brass candelabra and dark wooden furniture, and is wildly popular with the fashion set.
Tollbugata 24, T 2283 7228, mauds.no

Sverre Sætre
This avant-garde *konditori* is the domain of Norwegian pastry chef Sverre Sætre, who trained at the Michelin-starred Bagatelle (T 2212 1440) across town before opening his eponymous pâtisserie in 2008. The mouthwatering confectionery is delicately handmade on site — try the sweet/savoury combinations, such as Sætre's signature 'dry cakes' (puff pastry with red peppers and Parmesan) — while the specialist preserves make excellent presents. Visually it's a treat too, with laboratory-like stainless-steel-and-glass display cases teamed with cabinets of aged Norwegian oak. An adjoining room houses Robert Thoresen's Kaffa Butikk (T 2244 3536), which sells coffee by the cup (standing room only) and gourmet beans.
Niels Juels gate 70b, T 2244 5400, www.sverreskonditori.no

Nodee

As one of the only high-end Asian eateries in town, Nodee has been a hit ever since opening in 2003. Its popularity is well deserved. The kitchen is run by Hong Kong-born chef Man Lung Chen and the enterprising menu features wok dishes that draw on pan-oriental influences, such as the Szechuan grilled fillet of beef and the now ubiquitous black cod. There's a sushi bar (above) that also does a great line in dim sum, and a low-ceilinged dining room with jute chairs, thick-pile carpets and patterned wallpaper that feels like an expensively furnished Upper East Side living room. Book ahead for the tables on the terrace, open from May to September. *Middelthunes gate 25, T 2293 3450, nodee.no*

Bølgen & Moi

This former electricity substation was built in 1942 by the Germans during their occupation, and has been transformed into an upmarket all-day canteen by Oslo's Dark Architects. Since opening in 2001, it has become a firm fixture with celebs, young professionals and socialites, who treat it as a home-from-home. Discreet staff glide around effortlessly, remembering everyone's favourite seats and serving up bistro classics, such as oven-baked halibut or slow-cooked veal. The look is scrubbed-up warehouse chic, with slate flooring, exposed brickwork and uncovered ventilation units. Leather benches, cushions, photographic prints and a large wood-fired oven used for pizzas provide the comfort factor.
Løvenskiolds gate 26, T 2411 5353, bolgenogmoi.no

Alex Sushi

Dominating this minimalist Japanese restaurant is a super-busy oval-shaped teak sushi bar (above), where head chef Alex Cabiao has been rolling the finest (and most expensive) sashimi and sushi in town since 2001. His formative training in Tokyo is apparent in the emphasis on freshness and texture, and a menu that remains loyal to traditional Japanese cuisine with little in the way of Nobu-style fusion to appease the uninitiated. The crowd that gathers here night-in, night-out, is proof that Cabiao's no-nonsense approach has been warmly embraced. Try the Norwegian-sourced scallops and the king crab tempura maki.
Cort Adelers gate 2, T 2243 9999, alexsushi.no

Hos Thea

Situated on the ground floor of an elegant century-old townhouse, this was a highly regarded butcher before its conversion into Hos Thea (Thea's House) in 1987. Offering accomplished cooking without the usual formalities and fanfare, choice dishes include Norwegian duck breast in *vigneronne* sauce or cod with fried chorizo. Refurbished in 2006 by designer Helene Heine, the interior is a study in understated luxe; a calming palette of white, cream and brown, with starched table linen, silver cutlery and crystal glassware. A small but well-proportioned space, it has the intimate, hushed feel of a private dining room.
Gabels gate 11, T 2244 6874, hosthea.no

Etoile Bar
The hotel bar on the top floor of the Grand (see p026) has a reputation as a chic all-day meeting spot. Designed by Berit Trengereid and Hanne Hovland Sternes, its colourfully upholstered sofas and armchairs are bathed in light that streams through the slanted floor-to-ceiling windows. The informal daytime menu is perfect for on-the-hoof dining, and consists of simple open sandwiches and salads, such as king crab with avocado and burnt black pepper. By night there is a cocktail lounge vibe, and locals sip espresso martinis before hitting the smart clubs in nearby Solli plass.
Karl Johans gate 31, T 2321 2000, grand.no

Sult

This eaterie has managed to maintain its edgy vibe ever since opening in 1996 and has become something of a stalwart in hip Grünerløkka. The compact dining room was given a glossy makeover in 2007 by artist Ingvild Wærhaug, who added slate floors, glass-covered pop art tables and a tilted shelving unit that shows off a well-chosen wine selection. Head chef Andre Wrængbø's menu extols the virtues of *nynorsk* (new Norwegian) cuisine and includes dishes such as blue mussels with tomatoes, lime zest and croutons. The weekend-only lunch service is popular, so book ahead. The adjoining bar Tørst heaves with a sharply dressed crowd.
*Thorvald Meyers gate 26,
T 2287 0467, sult.no*

No 15

This stylish brasserie is a haunt of west Oslo's party set and features a bling bar, crystal chandelier, ornate cornicing and shabby-chic furniture. The kitchen turns out faultlessly executed and generously proportioned dishes such as the signature steak No 15, which will set you up for the night, as the venue turns into a DJ-led cocktail lounge with a pre-club vibe.
Skovveien 15, T 2255 0315, no-15.no

URBAN LIFE

Klosteret

This charming restaurant outpost opened in 1992 and sits in an increasingly kooky neighbourhood near the northern end of Hausmanns gate. Its exposed brick walls, wrought-iron chairs and antique rugs make the cosy, candlelit basement a wonderful place to be ensconced for a long, lingering dinner. Head chef Daniel Karlson offers a modern Norwegian menu built around hearty, regionally sourced, seasonal produce that is the perfect foil for dark winter evenings. Try the grilled scallops with mango and lime chutney followed by pheasant with cep tagliatelle.
Fredensborgveien 13, T 2335 4900, klosteret.no

Internasjonalen

This much-fêted watering hole is slightly dated but has a certain grungy charm. Originally just a boxy ground-floor room with a large retro-style bar, a much-needed refit in 2009 saw the addition of a larger upstairs area for gigs that attracts big-name European acts, thanks to Internasjonalen's links with the annual Øya festival. The patchy service doesn't deter a loyal following, thanks to its legendary cocktails and location on the south-west corner of Youngstorget. The bar is part of the holy trinity for alternative, music-loving hipsters, along with the nearby Café Mono (T 2241 4166) and Fisk og Vilt (Pløens gate 1).
Youngstorget 2, T 4000 4277, internasjonalen.no

La Belle Sole

Behind an unassuming, listed Jugendstil façade lies a deceptively large and labyrinthine nightspot, which twists and turns, taking in a VIP lounge and several bars. In the centre you'll find a sizeable dancefloor, which is serviced by some of Europe's top DJs. The crowd is a mix of platinum blondes in Pucci-print dresses and besuited guys ordering the house cocktail, a Grey Goose martini. The décor is intentionally over-the-top and has a decadent late-1980s New York warehouse feel with concrete floors and an eclectic mix of luxurious textiles and bejewelled light fixtures. But it's the low-level sofas, dark nooks and unisex loos that give this club its louche disco feel and its patrons a reputation to match. An alternative clubbing option is to cross town for an edgier vibe at Revolver (T 9572 1303).
Observatoriegaten 2b, T 2255 4000, labellesole.no

061

URBAN LIFE

INSIDER'S GUIDE
JULIE ANN SEGLEM, BOUTIQUE OWNER

Originally from the small town of Lyngdal on Norway's south coast, Julie Ann Seglem moved to the capital four years ago and co-owns Sjarm (see p074) with Veslemøy Kvamme. It's located in Grünerløkka, an area she describes as the city's 'beating creative heart', but Seglem chooses to live in Majorstuen, 'right on the edge of Frognerparken, where it's tranquil and quiet'. In the mornings, she likes to go for a run through the park, often treating herself to a chocolate scone from United Bakeries (see p033) afterwards. For clothes she is a fan of Little Miss T (Søndre gate 12a, T 9183 2227) and G-Oslo (Welhavens gate 18, T 2246 8188). Midweek she meets friends at Olympen Mat & Vinhus (see p045), 'laughing and eating into the night', while Seglem's ideal Friday evening is an intimate dinner at Palace Grill (Solligata 2, T 2313 1140), 'if I'm lucky enough to bag a table', before moving on to Tørst (see p055).

Weekends start with a strong espresso at Java (Ullevålsveien 47a, T 2246 0800) and a stroll around St Hanshaugen park. She likes to pop into Samlersenteret (see p076) to 'rummage around for old books and careworn trinkets' before spending a pleasant afternoon lounging in Oslo Mekaniske Verksted (see p040). Special occasions call for a reservation at Restaurant Oscarsgate (see p040) or 34 Restaurant (34th floor, Radisson SAS Plaza Hotel, Sonja Henies plass 3, T 2205 8000) for the 'breathtaking view'.
For full addresses, see Resources.

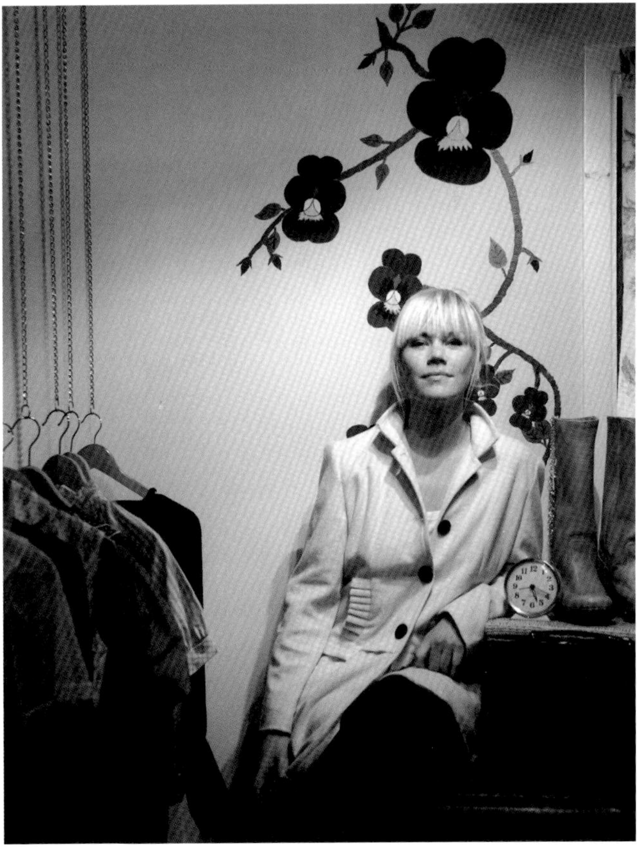

ARCHITOUR
A GUIDE TO OSLO'S ICONIC BUILDINGS

Two distinct phases of architecture are apparent in Oslo's history. From the 1810s to the 1870s (known as the nation-building era), the neoclassical style dominated, heavily influenced by the Danes, as can be seen in Christian Heinrich Grosch's 1859 University of Oslo (Karl Johans gate 47), the 1819 Stock Exchange (Tollbugata 2) and the 1849 Royal Palace (Henrik Ibsens gate 1, T 2204 8700). In the 1930s, Bauhaus-inspired functionalism took hold and Oslo boasts delights such as the 1930 Kunstnernes Hus (Wergelandsveien 17, T 2285 3410), by Gudolf Blakstad and Herman Munthe-Kaas, the Rådhuset (see p068), Bislett Stadion (see p090) and the NRK Radiohuset (Bjørnstjerne Bjørnsons plass 1, T 2304 7000), by Nils Holter, which was built between 1938 and 1950.

Yet for a European capital, Oslo has been notoriously reticent about new builds ever since WWII, dragging its heels over the few projects that were approved, with the notable exception of the Aker Brygge area. All that is now changing with Fjord City, which will see 225 hectares of waterfront redeveloped, from Ormsund in the east to Frognerkilen in the west. Joining the Operahuset (see p010) in 2012 will be Renzo Piano's premises for the Astrup Fearnley Museum of Modern Art; a new joint home for the Munch Museum and Stenersen Museum, slated to open in 2013; as well as major housing schemes in Bjørvik, Skøyen and Filipstad.
For full addresses, see Resources.

Oslo International School
In 2006, Oslo-based architects Jarmund/ Vigsnæs began a renovation of Oslo International School, with the final phase due to be completed in autumn 2009, comprising a new auditorium, gym and drama and music facilities. Security has also been taken into consideration, with a rubber asphalt playground enclosed within a new wing for primary students. The striped, multicoloured fibre-cement panels are a reflection of the diversity of the student body, which is composed of more than 50 nationalities. Jarmund/ Vigsnæs previously transformed a former factory into a light-filled glass box for the Oslo School of Architecture and Design (T 2299 7000), which opened in 2002 at Maridalsveien 29.
Gamle Ringeriksvei 53,
www.oslointernationalschool.no

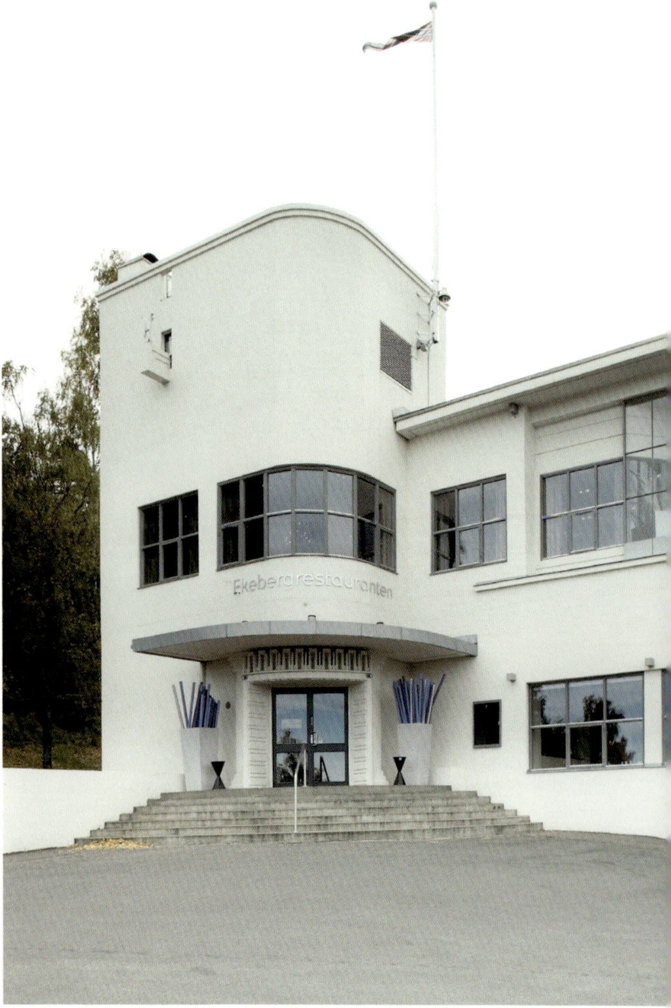
Ekebergrestauranten

Ekeberg Restaurant
This functionalist gem in the south-eastern hills was financed by a tobacco company and opened in 1916. A competition for its redesign was won by Oslo-based architect Lars Backer in 1927. His vision was realised in 1929, and the public flocked to enjoy sweeping views from the veranda. The restaurant fell into disrepair and had closed by the late 1990s, only to be revived when businessman Christian Ringnes, property developer Eiendomsspar and restaurateur Bjørn Tore Furset announced a major renovation led by Thomas Ness of Radius Design. The reddish-brown terrazzo floors and steel-frame windows were restored, and reproduction furniture was custom-made. An upper-floor fireplace was realised from Backer's original drawings, a feature he was unable to complete at the time.
Kongsveien 15, T 2324 2300, ekebergrestauranten.com

Rådhuset

As well as housing the Oslo council, the double-towered Rådhuset (City Hall) is also a public gallery space, with murals, tapestries, wood carvings and sculptures on display. Designed by Arnstein Arneberg and Magnus Poulsson in 1930, construction was disrupted by WWII and the red-brick building was not inaugurated until 1950, coinciding with celebrations to mark the city's 950th anniversary. The cast-bronze 38-bell carillon was added to the east tower in 1952, and just for good measure, 11 extra bells were added in 2000. The Great Hall is the venue for the Nobel Peace Prize ceremony, which takes place annually on 10 December. The raised walkways are the spiritual home of the city's skateboarding fraternity.
Rådhusplassen, T 8150 0606, oslo.kommune.no

Colosseum Kino
Opened in 1928, the then 2,100-seat cinema was the largest in Scandinavia. Designed by architects Jacob Hansen and Gerhard Iversen, its centrepiece is an impressive domed auditorium, more than 40m in diameter. It was hailed as one of Europe's most beautiful cinemas, but was devastated by fire during the premiere of *Mutiny on the Bounty* in 1963 and the dome collapsed. Architect Sverre Fehn restored the building and the venue reopened in 1964. Subsequent renovations and extensions, the last of which took place in 1998, haven't been kind to the interior. But despite the gaudy film billboards, the policeman's helmet-shaped copper roof has kept some of its lustre and adds a touch of splendour to the neighbourhood.
Fridtjof Nansens vei 6, T 9943 2000, oslokino.no

Mortensrud church
Designed by Jensen & Skodvin and completed in 2002, this modern church features a steel frame, dry slate walls, concrete floors and an orthogonal glass façade. Gunnar Torvund's stained-glass altar includes stones from Robben Island (where Nelson Mandela was imprisoned), Jerusalem and the Berlin Wall.
Helga Vaneks vei 15, T 2362 9980, mortensrud.no

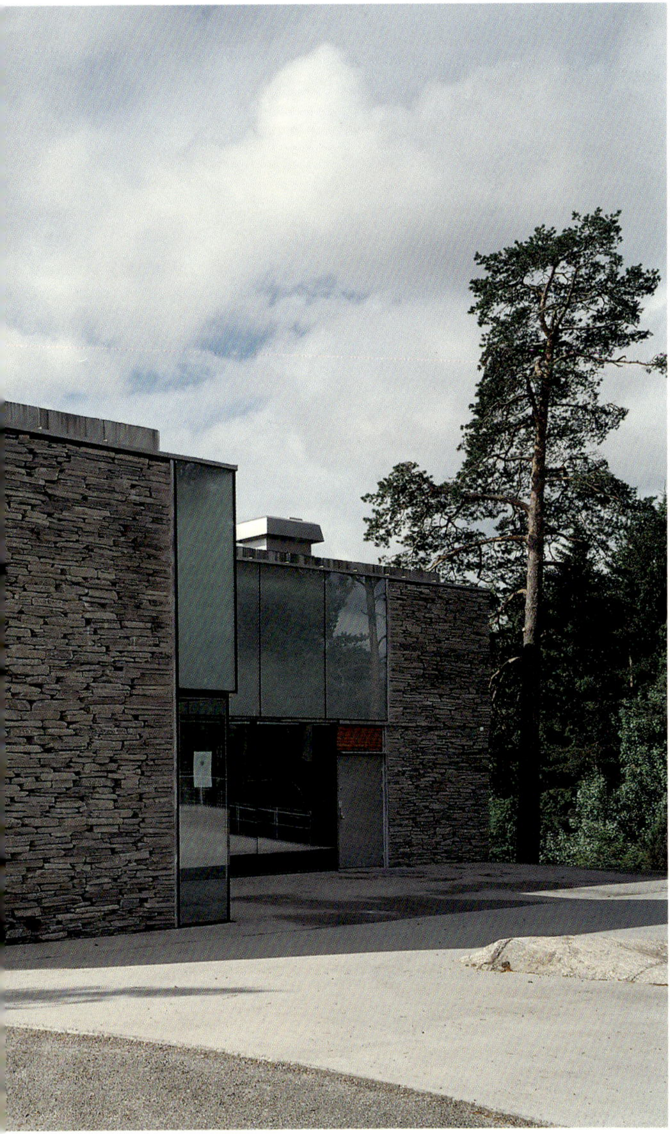

SHOPPING
THE BEST RETAIL THERAPY AND WHAT TO BUY

The past few years have seen an exponential rise in the number of independent stores in Oslo. City regulations have limited the development of large-scale shopping malls, to the benefit of the boutique scene, which is now thriving. On the design front there has been a resurgence of homegrown talent, and there is plenty of sleek furniture, reimagined household items and interesting gadgets to be found. Pur Norsk (Thereses gate 14, T 2246 4045) has a great selection of contemporary Norwegian-produced wares.

St Hanshaugen has an intriguing blend of womenswear outlets, upmarket delis and the antiques shop/bookstore Samlersenteret (see p076). In Marjorstuen, Fromagerie (Valkyriegata 9, T 2260 1995) sells delicious cheeses, cured meats and smoked salmon from specialist farms, and on Bogstadsveien, the swankiest retail avenue in town, search the boutiques for fledgling but forward-thinking Norwegian labels Batlak og Selvig (batlakogselvig.com), Arne & Carlos (arne-carlos.com) and Iselin Engan (iselinengan.com). Here you will also find the Swedish brands Acne (Grønnegata 1, T 2259 4500) and Tiger of Sweden (Parkveien 25, T 2336 7710).

Quality winter and skiwear basics are well represented; Viking's trademark 'Slagbjørn' wellies are an Oslo classic. We're also fans of merino base layers from Devold and seam-sealed storm jackets from Norrøna, available at Intersport (Storgata 11, T 2331 0990). *For full addresses, see Resources.*

Sørensen Østlyngen Møbler
This store moved into Bygdøy allé from sleepy Briskeby in 2008 and has made the most of the increased showroom space. Spread over two floors, the all-white gallery-like shop showcases midcentury and contemporary furniture from Scandi designers, with a strong emphasis on Norwegian talent. On our visit, items on sale included the 'Peel' chair by Olav Eldøy for Variér, Hans Brattrud's 1957 'Scandia' chair, 'Tree' coatstands by Swedese and Roger Sveian's 'Eshu' sofa (all above). It's possible to commission bespoke pieces too. Nearby is Expo Nova Møbel (T 2313 1340), which also sells stylish urban furniture, although it is almost exclusively Italian.
Bygdøy allé 60, T 2256 3102, sorensenmobel.no

Sjarm

A hip, bohemian vibe pervades this Aladdin's cave of vintage clothes and accessories, mixed with contemporary fashion from local designers. It's laid out like a boudoir, with oak chests, art deco lamps, chandeliers and 1950s-style screens, all for sale, with Norwegian folk-pop playing in the background. It's the perfect ambience in which to peruse the exquisite dresses, sheepskin gilets, cowboy boots, beaded handbags and embroidered clutches, as well as the handcrafted jewellery made from onyx, white agate, porcelain and pearls. Sjarm can create bespoke items and has a selection of vintage bridalwear that can be customised to order. The nearby sister shop (T 2237 1932) focuses on furniture and homewares, and is equally charming.
Markveien 56, T 2235 0150, sjarm.biz

Moods of Norway

Childhood friends and fashion designers Simen Staalnacke and Peder Børresen opened Moods in 2003, and it has been so successful that an outpost is planned in Los Angeles. Divided into street, casual and cocktail sections, this is fashion that doesn't take itself too seriously, with myriad references to Staalnacke and Børresen's rural hometown of Stryn in west Norway. The flagship store even has a full-size tractor front painted gold and changing rooms that are kitted out to look like Staalnacke's grandmother's *hytte* (summer cabin). As you wander around Oslo, you'll notice Moods' brightly coloured boxers peeking out all over the place.
Akersgata 18, T 4662 7796, moodsofnorway.com

Samlersenteret
This quirky 1950s-style shop is a veritable treasure trove of unusual objets d'art, antique Scandinavian glass, ceramics, handmade bone china, glazed teapots and pottery, silver and brass. Displayed on rows of rickety wooden shelves and cabinets, the curios sit beside rare and out-of-print books on design, architecture and photography. Students from the Oslo School of Architecture and Design (see p065) up the road frequently pop in looking for offbeat finds or inspiration, while an older generation drops by to trade stamps and coins. The shop is run by the knowledgeable Tor Mørch, an expert on books, and Knut Paulsrud, an antiques specialist and all-round raconteur.
Bjerregaards gate 13-15, T 2242 2240, samlersenteret.no

SHOPPING

Secret Society
The clean, stripped-back boutique Secret Society is located in a converted bakery, which is appropriately hidden down a residential-looking alley. Owner Fanny Jahre has quickly established a loyal client base among Oslo's twentysomething fashionistas, who appreciate her well-edited selection of both mens- and womenswear by Norwegian favourites Arne & Carlos, and international brands such as 18th Amendment, Helmut Lang, Junya Watanabe and Martin Margiela. Also look out for statement jewellery and accessories, including Natalie Brilli's soft leatherwork. This place is so spot on we wish we could have kept it a secret.
Briskebyveien 38, T 9139 5667, secretsociety.no

Damms Antikvariat

This store has been dealing in rare books, maps and prints for more than 160 years since Niels Wilhelm Damm opened for business in 1843 in Grønland. In 1996 the shop relocated to this modern glass building designed by Torstein Ramberg in one of Oslo's historic squares. English-language first editions to be found here include Charles Dickens' *Our Mutual Friend* from 1865. Norwegians hold literature in high regard. Local beatniks are drawn to independent bookstore Tronsmo (T 2299 0399), which specialises in foreign affairs and photography, while Litteraturhuset (T 2295 5530), located by the Slottsparken and inaugurated in 2007, has hosted talks by authors Zadie Smith, Siri Hustvedt and Hanif Kureishi, and boasts an inviting café and terrace. *Akersgaten 2, T 2241 0402, damms.no*

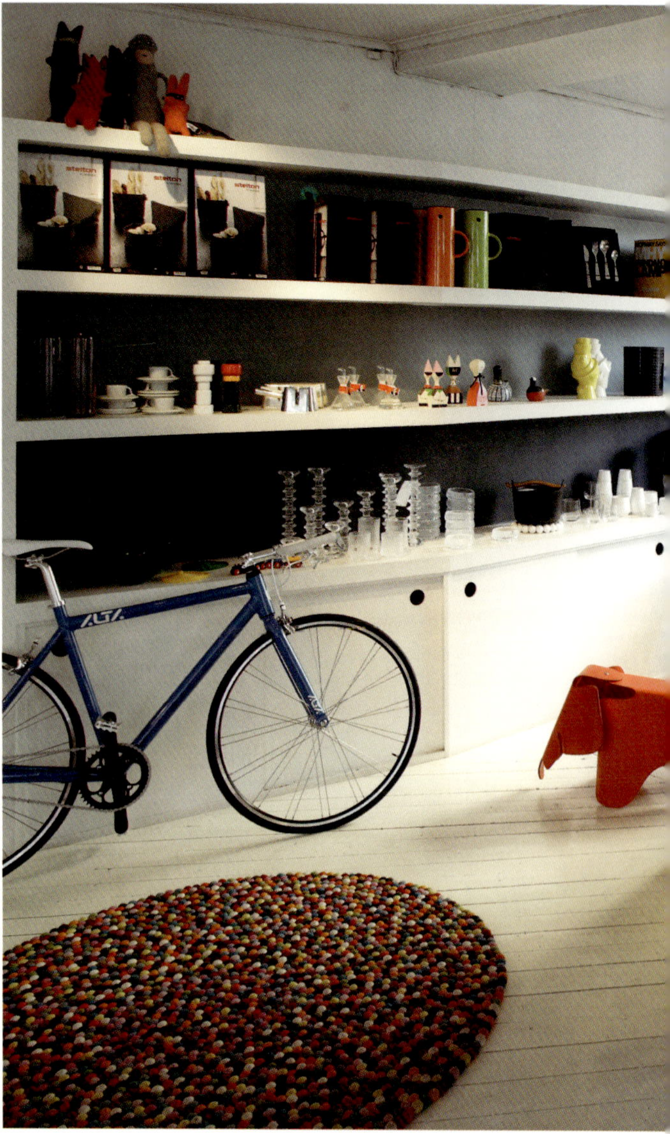
stelton
stelton
stelton

Norway Says
Product designers Andreas Engesvik, Torbjørn Andersen and Espen Voll opened this retail/studio space in 2002. Their clean, innovative, often award-winning work includes the Alta bike (pictured) – a collaboration – a hit with style-savvy Oslo commuters. Also on sale are pieces by Tom Dixon, Iittala, Stelton and Vitra. *Thorvald Meyers gate 15, T 2238 2577, norwaysaysshop.no*

Norske Grafikere

This bijou shop/art gallery is run by the Association of Norwegian Printmakers, which celebrated its 90th anniversary in 2009. It was founded by Edvard Munch, Harald Sohlberg and Erik Werenskiold and represents more than 300 artists, with at least 4,000 pieces archived on site available for purchase; many prints, lithographs, illustrations and reliefs are reasonably priced. Rising stars on the Norwegian scene include Hanna Boyesen, Pauliina Gauffin and Lars Teigum. The gallery puts on regular exhibitions.
Tollbugaten 24, T 2335 8940, norske-grafikere.no

Hunting Lodge

Welshmen Dafydd Jones and Mark James, whose backgrounds are in product design, music and fashion, opened this design-led store/gallery in 2007. Edgy streetwear and ironic tees are complemented by art books, boys' toys and accessories, and there are plenty of cult labels, such as Dan Macmillan's Zoltar. Even the presentation style is original, and many of the Lodge's fixtures are one-off designs themselves, such as the cute 'Antler' shelving system (above). Downstairs is an exhibition space, Hide, showcasing up-and-coming Norwegian artists and graphic designers.
Torggata 36, T 9987 0455, huntinglodge.no

Shabby

Just around the corner from Uranienborg church, this elegant and stylish interiors shop opened in 2003, selling handcrafted north European furniture, Persian rugs, Indian wicker chairs, vintage bathroom furniture and mirrors, linen cushions, cashmere blankets and lambswool throws. The spacious store has a soothing colour palette of slate, oatmeal and chestnut, in which it also sells limited-edition accessories, such as handmade scarves, and a range of organic soap and perfume. Much of the stock is sourced by co-owner Alexandra Villefrance on regular trips to France, Belgium and Sweden.
Niels Juels gate 51, T 2255 7000,
www.shabby.no

Passiflora

This independent florist is a favourite of Princess Mette-Marit, who commissioned her wedding flowers here, and supplies hotels such as the Grims Grenka (see p017). In full bloom, it is one of the loveliest spaces in town, but for visitors, the reason to pop by this wood-panelled shop is to peruse the antique garden furniture and wrought-iron birdcages sourced by owner Aina Nyberget Kleppe. The handmade oversized scented candles from Denmark make great gifts, as do the vintage Italian clay pots.
Skovveien 16, T 2255 6378,
www.passiflora.no

980

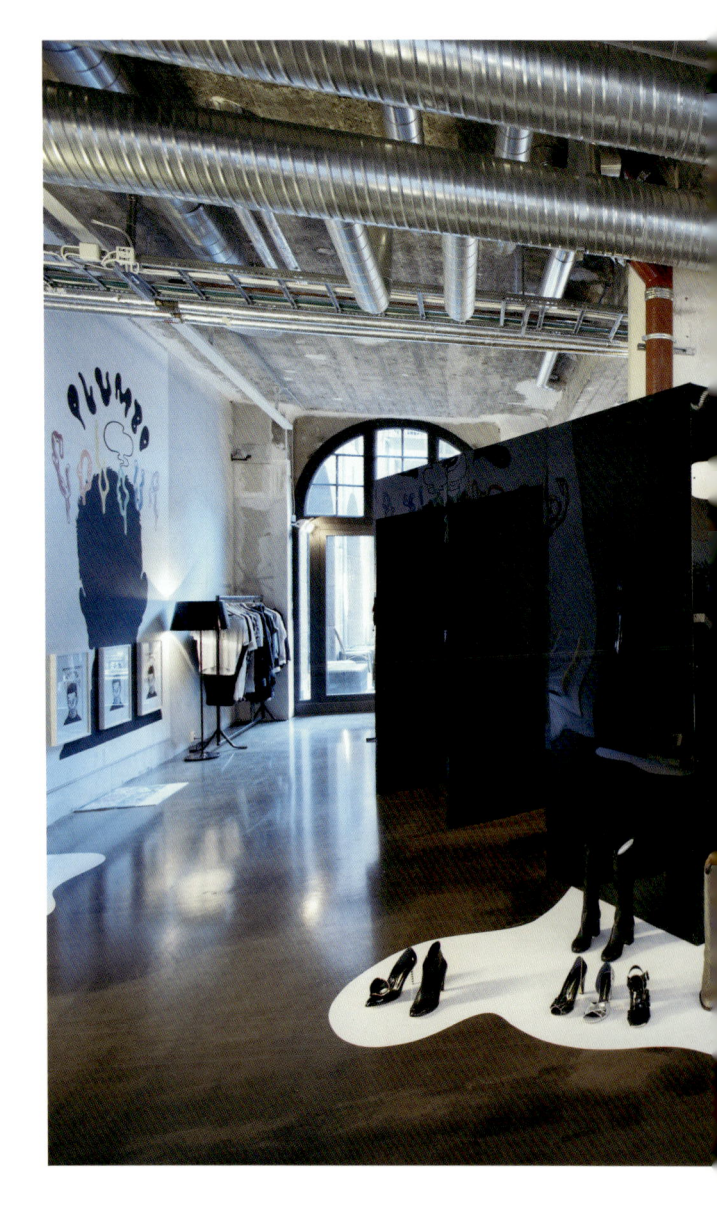

Freudian Kicks
Interiors here are inspired by a pinball machine with movable black acrylic panels and rails displaying urbanwear by north European labels such as Sneaky Steve, Wood Wood, Best Behavior, APC and Kokon To Zai. Books, gadgets and jewellery are also on sale, and there are regular installations and DJ happenings.
Prinsens gate 10b, T 2242 9300, freudiankicks.no

SPORTS AND SPAS
WORK OUT, CHILL OUT OR JUST WATCH

One of Oslo's best features is the ease with which one can swap the urban environment for the natural wilderness, with water-based pleasures off the idyllic islands dotted around the Oslofjord and winter sports in the hills just outside the city centre.

Frognerparken attracts armies of joggers but it also boasts six clay tennis courts and Frognerbadet (Middelthuns gate 28, T 2327 5450), a modernised 1956 lido with three pools. If it's a more pampered dip you seek, try the subterranean Snøhetta-designed Artesia Spa (Majorstuveien 36, T 2293 3550) or its sister branch in the Grand Hotel (see p094). Alternatively, take a ferry-bus from Vippetangen, south-east of Akershus Castle (see p009), to one of the six main islands in the bay. Our favourite is Gressholmen, which has many coves that are perfect for a picnic and a paddle.

A popular weekend hike is from Holmenkollen station up to Ullevålseter, high above the city, and back down to Sognsvann Lake to rejoin the T-bane. The nearby Nordmarka Forest is criss-crossed by mountain bike trails, and during the winter it becomes a haven for cross-country skiers; you can hire equipment from Skiservice cabins, such as the one behind Voksenkollen station (Tomm Murstadbakken 2, T 2213 9500). Also in this area is the Tryvann Vinterpark (T 4046 2700), a modern alpine facility with 14 landscaped slopes that attracts urban skiers and snowboarders. *For full addresses, see Resources.*

City Bikes
The communal bicycle scheme that rolled out in 2002 has become part of everyday life in Oslo. Thanks to the city's relatively small size and the civic-minded attitude of its drivers towards cyclists, locals have taken to it with zeal. To use the service, register for an electronic Smart Card, offered to tourists for £7 per day, swipe and go. You can return your four-speed blue-and-white Smart Bike, designed by Oslo-based industrial design firm Frost Produkt, to any of the many stands, such as the one at the intersection of Prinsens gate and Dronningens gate (above).
T 8150 0250, oslobysykkel.no

Bislett Stadion
This functionalist concrete stadium was designed by Frode Rinnan and finished in 1940 and hosted many international speed-skating championships. However, after more than six decades of use it was torn down and totally rebuilt to a similar design by Danish architects CF Møller. Reopened in 2005, it is now used for football matches and athletics meets.
Bislettgata, T 2346 2000

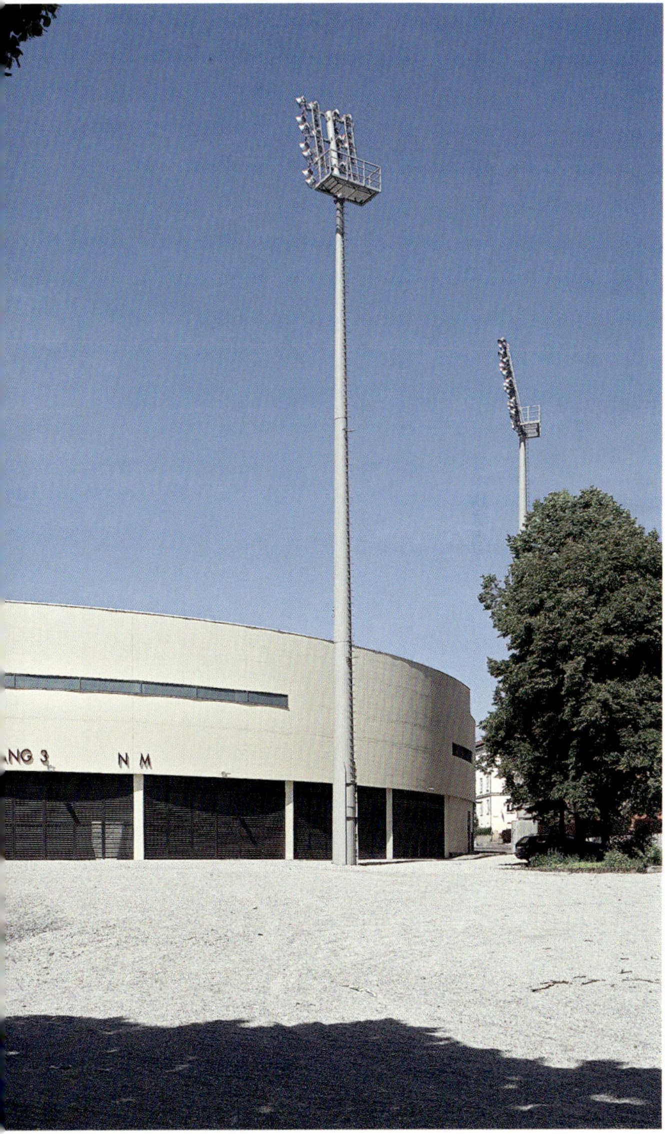

Barber & Friseursalongen
This old-fashioned gentlemen's barber was once located in the lobby of the Hugustin Hotel, which closed in 1920. The salon remained and its authentic charm lives on in the original mirrors, 1930s chairs from Chicago and antique cash register. These days, pinstriped (but open-necked) Norwegian businessmen drop by for a chat and quick trim before lunching next door at Mauds (see p048), as do sharp young blades sporting impressive beards that need taming. High-concept, unisex styling alternatives include Hope Hair (T 2241 4140), with its revitalising Shu Uemura treatments, and the independent Dugg, which offers organic hair colouring at its outlets in Frogner (T 2255 6500) and Grünerløkka (T 2323 0515).
Tollbugaten 24, T 2241 1818

093

SPORTS

Artesia Spa
Located on the eighth floor of the Grand Hotel (see p026), the main draw of this 450 sq m facility is the stunning pool, which is clad in black tiles, lined with a row of birch tree trunks and bathed in atmospheric light. It evokes a night-time dip in a remote lake. Treatments include a Norwegian Seaweed Cocoon and others using Ole Henriksen products.
Karl Johans gate 31, T 2282 5000, grand.no

095

SPORTS

ESCAPES

WHERE TO GO IF YOU WANT TO LEAVE TOWN

Oslo-ites will often regale you with tales of idyllic childhoods spent in the Norwegian countryside. Get some idea of what they are talking about by hiring a car and driving along the scenic south coast, with its secluded sandy beaches and *hytte*-dotted fishing villages. One of the most picturesque, Filtvet, is home to Villa Malla (opposite), a destination restaurant run by the highly regarded chef Sonja Lee that's worth building a leisurely weekend around.

A well-worn jaunt is to Norway's second city, Bergen (see p100), situated on the west coast. It's surrounded by brooding mountains and has a reputation for rain, but in the summer it benefits from the Gulf Stream, which generates balmy temperatures rarely associated with Scandinavia. In the late Middle Ages Bergen was a principal port of the Hanseatic League and it has a well-preserved history. There is an overnight sleeper train from Oslo, although it's a shame to miss the breathtaking journey across Hordaland and the rugged scenery of Hardangervidda National Park.

For a more ambitious escape, from late 2009 a two-hour flight north will take you to The Other Side (Neiden, T 78 996 8203), a boutique hotel on the isolated Neiden Plateau, close to the Finnish-Russian border, which gives new meaning to getting away from it all. Designed by the Paris-based Swedish-French firm Ralston & Bau, this is a very stylish way to experience the Northern Lights. *For full addresses, see Resources.*

Villa Malla, Filtvet, Hurum
The slickest way to access this chic seafront hideaway in Filtvet is from Aker Brygge, where you can catch a boat that will whizz you down the Oslofjord within an hour. In summer, grab a seat on the terrace (above) to enjoy owner-chef Sonja Lee's modern brand of pan-Mediterranean cuisine. Lee was head chef at Damien Hirst's Pharmacy in London in the late 1990s and won plaudits for Magma, her former eaterie in Oslo. Inside Villa Malla, the white walls, polished concrete floors and sandalwood furniture allow the views to take centre stage. The season runs from mid-March to December. Lee has plans for two guesthouses on site, which are scheduled for completion in late 2010.
Stranda 3, T 3279 5090, villamalla.no

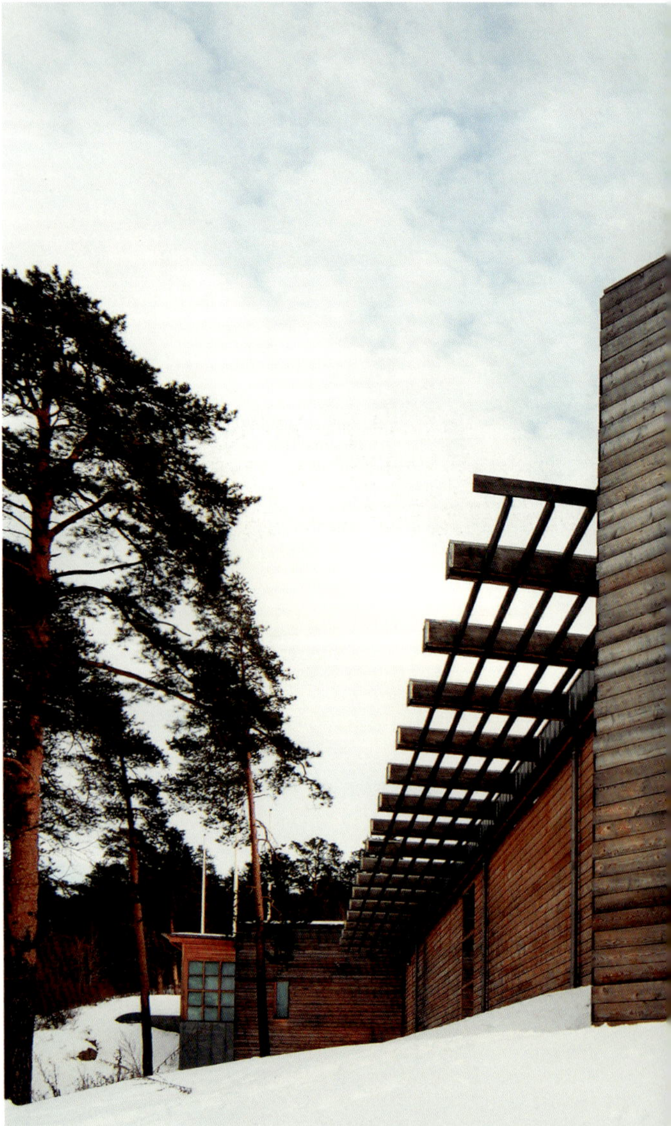

Henie Onstad Art Centre
This modern art museum opened in 1968 in an expressionist building by architects Jon Eikvar and Sven-Erik Engebretsen, who also designed an extension in 1994. The D-shaped, Siberian larch-clad Haaken Wing (pictured), by Stein Halvorsen, was opened in 2003. It is all set in a sculpture park on a peninsula in the Oslofjord.
Sonja Henies vei 31, Høvikodden,
T 6780 4880, hok.no

Bergen Art Museum
Comprising three buildings that line Lille Lungegård lake, this museum is home to several of Edvard Munch's masterpieces. The Lysverket building (above) melds art deco, functionalist and neoclassical styles and was designed by Fredrik Arnesen and Arthur Darre Kaarbø. Opened in 1939 as the electricity board HQ, it was converted into a gallery in 2003. Bergen was Norway's capital from 1217 to 1299 and its historic Bryggen wharf is a big draw, but the 1930s functionalist architecture is also superb, notably Leif Kuhnle Grung's Blaauwgården (Christian Sundts gate 1) and Per Grieg's Sundt department store (Torgallmenningen 14). Dine at the outstanding Restaurant Potetkjelleren (T 5532 0070), once a potato cellar that dates back to the 15th century.
Rasmus Meyers allé 9, Bergen,
T 5556 8000, bergenartmuseum.no

Juvet Landscape Hotel, Valldal
Deep in the wilderness of west Norway's forests and fjords, this eco resort is located in the grounds of a 16th-century farm and comprises freestanding cube-like studios and a separate spa in a converted barn with a hot tub and sauna. Opened in June 2009, the hotel has been cleverly integrated into the natural surroundings by architects Jensen & Skodvin, using locally sourced pine and walls of smoked glass. Immaculately designed interiors feature Toshiyuki Kita's 'Tok' lounge chairs (above), which are positioned to make the most of the views. Activities include ice-climbing on the Trollstigen glacier, hiking in Reinheimen national park and whitewater rafting. To get here take the 45-minute flight to Ålesund, and then transfer by speedboat.
Alstad, T 7025 8652, juvet.com

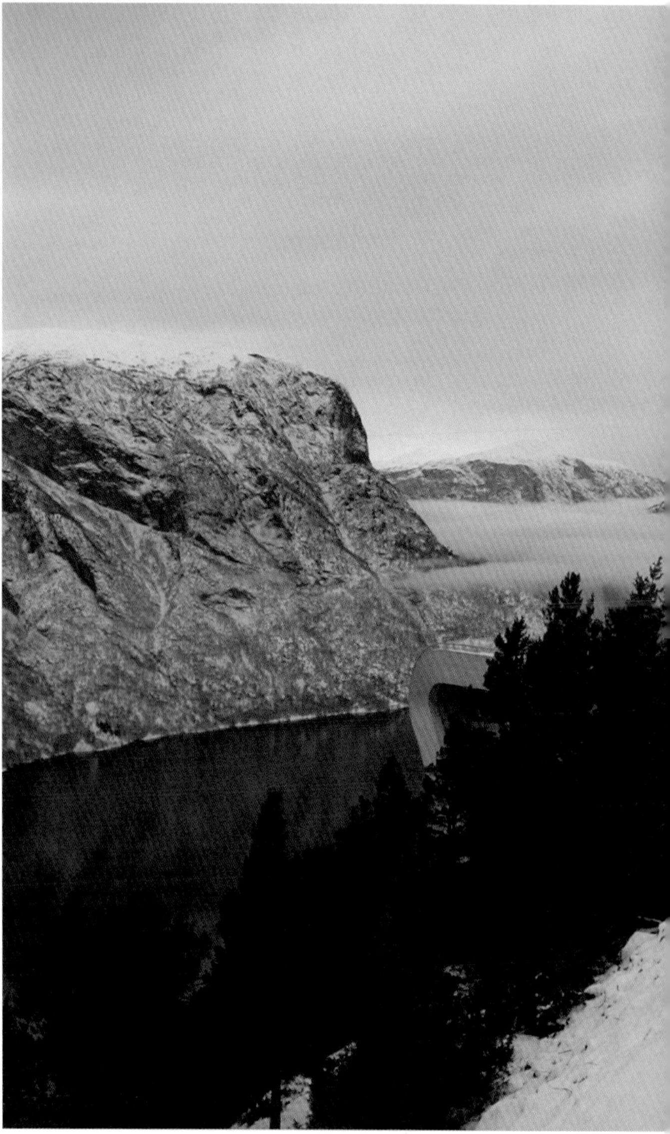

Aurland lookout, Flåm Valley
Another way to see the western fjords is to survey the landscape from architects Todd Saunders and Tommie Wilhelmsen's lookout, five hours' drive from Oslo. A steel frame clad in timber, it has the terrifying feel of a 600m diving board. Closer to town, the six-hour hike over Besseggen ridge affords views of the royal blue Bessvatnet lake on one side and the emerald Gjende on the other.

NOTES
SKETCHES AND MEMOS

ICEBAR OSLO – KRISTIAN IV'S GATE 12. FRI 15X01. SAT 12X01

TUE SENSE – HENRIK IBSENS GATE 4. FRI 16X03. SAT 20X03

RESOURCES
CITY GUIDE DIRECTORY

A

Acne 072
 Grønnegata 1
 T 2259 4500
 acnestudios.com

Akershus Castle 009
 Akershus festning
 T 2309 3553

Alex Sushi 052
 Cort Adelers gate 2
 T 2243 9999
 alexsushi.no

Åpent Bakeri Plaza 043
 Damplassen 24-25
 T 2204 9667
 apentbakeri.no

Det Åpne Teater 040
 Tøyenbekken 34
 T 2205 2800
 www.detapneteater.no

Artesia Spa 094
 Grand Hotel
 Karl Johans gate 31
 T 2282 5000
 grand.no
 Majorstuveien 36
 T 2293 3550
 artesia.no

Astrup Fearnley Museum of Modern Art 064
 Dronningens gate 4
 T 2293 6060
 afmuseet.no

Aurland lookout 102
 Aurland
 Flåm Valley

B

Barber & Friseursalongen 092
 Tollbugaten 24
 T 2241 1818

Bagatelle 049
 Bygdøy allé 3
 T 2212 1440
 bagatelle.no

Barbeint 032
 Henrik Ibsens gate 60a
 T 9506 4686
 barbeint-oslo.no

La Belle Sole 060
 Observatoriegaten 2b
 T 2255 4000
 labellesole.no

Bergen Art Museum 100
 Rasmus Meyers allé 9
 Bergen
 T 5556 8000
 bergenartmuseum.no

Bislett Stadion 090
 Bislettgata
 T 2346 2000
 idrettsetaten.oslo.kommune.no/
 bislett_stadion

Blå 040
 Brenneriveien 9c
 T 4000 4277
 blaaoslo.no

Blaauwgården 100
 Christian Sundts gate 1
 Bergen

Bølgen & Moi 051
 Løvenskiolds gate 26
 T 2411 5353
 bolgenogmoi.no

C

Café Mono 059
Pløens gate 4
T 2241 4166
cafemono.no

City Bikes 089
T 8150 0250
oslobysykkel.no

Colosseum Kino 069
Fridtjof Nansens vei 6
T 9943 2000
oslokino.no

D

Damms Antikvariat 079
Akersgaten 2
T 2241 0402
damms.no

Dattera til Hagen 040
Grønland 10
T 2217 1861
dattera.no

Dugg 092
Bygdøy allé 51b
T 2255 6500
Thorvald Meyers gate 25
T 2323 0515
dugg.no

E

Ekeberg Restaurant 066
Kongsveien 15
T 2324 2300
ekebergrestauranten.com

Emanuel Vigeland Museum 009
Grimelundsveien 8
T 2214 5788
emanuelvigeland.museum.no

Etoile Bar 054
Grand Hotel
Karl Johans gate 31
T 2321 2000
grand.no

Expo Nova Møbel 073
Bygdøy allé 69
T 2313 1340
expo-nova.no

F

Fisk og Vilt 059
Pløens gate 1

Freudian Kicks 086
Prinsens gate 10b
T 2242 9300
freudiankicks.no

Frognerbadet 088
Middelthuns gate 28
T 2327 5450

Fromagerie 072
Valkyriegata 9
T 2260 1995

G

Gamle Aker church 012
Akersbakken 26
T 2362 9120
gamle-aker.no

G-Oslo 062
Welhavens gate 18
T 2246 8188

Grand Café 035
 Grand Hotel
 Karl Johans gate 31
 T 2321 2018
 grand.no

H
Henie Onstad Art Centre 098
 Sonja Henies vei 31
 Høvikodden
 T 6780 4880
 hok.no
Holmenkollen ski jump 009
 Kongeveien 5
 T 2292 3200
Hope Hair 092
 Prinsensgate 8
 T 2241 4140
Hos Thea 053
 Gabels gate 11
 T 2244 6874
 hosthea.no
Hunting Lodge 083
 Torggata 36
 T 9987 0455
 huntinglodge.no

I
Internasjonalen 059
 Youngstorget 2
 T 4000 4277
 internasjonalen.no
Intersport 072
 Storgata 11
 T 2331 0990

J
Java 062
 Ullevålsveien 47a
 T 2246 0800

K
Kaffa Butikk 049
 Niels Juels gate 70
 T 2244 3536
 kaffa.no
Kampen Bistro 040
 Bøgata 21
 T 2219 7708
 kampenbistro.no
Klosteret 058
 Fredensborgveien 13
 T 2335 4900
 klosteret.no
Kunstnernes Hus 064
 Wergelandsveien 17
 T 2285 3410
 kunstnerneshus.no

L
Litteraturhuset 079
 Wergelandsveien 29
 T 2295 5530
 litteraturhuset.no
Little Miss T 062
 Søndre gate 12a
 T 9183 2227
Lofoten Fiskerestaurant 044
 Stranden 75
 T 2283 0808
 www.lofoten-fiskerestaurant.no

M
Mauds 048
 Tollbugata 24
 T 2283 7228
 mauds.no
Moods of Norway 075
 Akersgata 18
 T 4662 7796
 moodsofnorway.com
Mortensrud church 070
 Helga Vaneks vei 15
 T 2362 9980
 mortensrud.no
Munch Museum 064
 Tøyengata 53
 T 2349 3500
 www.munch.museum.no
Museum of Contemporary Art 032
 Bankplassen 4
 T 2198 2000
 nationalmuseum.no

N
**National Museum
 of Architecture** 034
 Bankplassen 3
 T 2198 2100
 nationalmuseum.no
Nationaltheatret 014
 Johanne Dybwads plass 1
 T 2200 1400
 nationaltheatret.no
Nobel Peace Center 036
 Rådhusplassen
 T 4830 1000
 www.nobelpeacecenter.org
Nodee 050
 Middelthunes gate 25
 T 2293 3450
 nodee.no

No 15 056
 Skovveien 15
 T 2255 0315
 no-15.no
Norske Grafikere 082
 Tollbugaten 24
 T 2335 8940
 norske-grafikere.no
Norway Says 080
 Thorvald Meyers gate 15
 T 2238 2577
 norwaysaysshop.no
**Norwegian Centre for Design
 and Architecture** 032
 Hausmanns gate 16
 T 2329 2870
 doga.no
NRK Radiohuset 064
 Bjørnstjerne Bjørnsons plass 1
 T 2304 7000
 nrk.no

O
Olympen Mat & Vinhus 045
 Grønlandsleiret 15
 T 2410 1999
 olympen.no
Operahuset 010
 Kirsten Flagstads plass 1
 T 2142 2100
 www.operaen.no
Oslo International School 065
 Gamle Ringeriksvei 53
 www.oslointernationalschool.no

Oslo Mekaniske Verksted 040
Tøyenbekken 34
T 4523 7534
oslomekaniskeverksted.no
Oslo School of Architecture and Design 065
Maridalsveien 29
T 2299 7000
aho.no

P
Palace Grill 062
Solligata 2
T 2313 1140
www.palacegrill.no
Pascal Café 041
Tollbugata 11
T 2242 1119
pascal.no
Pascal Café de la Paix 041
Rådhusplassen
T 2283 0400
pascal.no
Passiflora 085
Skovveien 16
T 2255 6378
www.passiflora.no
Postgirobygget 009
Biskop Gunnerus gate 14
Posthallen 038
Prinsens gate 8
T 2241 1730
posthallenrestaurant.no
Pur Norsk 072
Thereses gate 14
T 2246 4045
purnorsk.com

R
Rådhuset 068
Rådhusplassen
T 8150 0606
oslo.kommune.no
Radisson SAS Plaza Hotel 009
Sonja Henies plass 3
T 2205 8000
plaza.oslo.radissonsas.com
Restaurant Oscarsgate 040
Inngang Pilestredet 63
T 2246 5906
restaurantoscarsgate.no
Restaurant Potetkjelleren 100
Kong Oscars gate 1a
Bergen
T 5532 0070
potetkjelleren.no
Revolver 060
Møllergata 32
T 9572 1303
revolveroslo.no
Royal Palace 064
Henrik Ibsens gate 1
T 2204 8700
www.kongehuset.no

S
Samlersenteret 076
Bjerregaards gate 13-15
T 2242 2240
samlersenteret.no
Secret Society 078
Briskebyveien 38
T 9139 5667
secretsociety.no

Shabby 084
Niels Juels gate 51
T 2255 7000
www.shabby.no
Sjarm 074
Markveien 56
T 2235 0150
Sofienberggata 6
T 2237 1932
sjarm.biz
Skiservice 088
Tomm Murstadbakken 2
T 2213 9500
skiservice.no
Sørensen Østlyngen Møbler 073
Bygdøy allé 60
T 2256 3102
sorensenmobel.no
Stenersen Museum 064
Munkedamsveien 15
T 2349 3600
stenersen.museum.no
Stock Exchange 064
Tollbugata 2
Südøst 037
Trondheimsveien 5
T 2335 3070
sydost.no
Sult 055
Thorvald Meyers gate 26
T 2287 0467
sult.no

Sundt 100
Torgallmenningen 14
Bergen
T 4166 1862
Sverre Sætre 049
Niels Juels gate 70b
T 2244 5400
www.sverreskonditori.no
SW20 042
Solligata 2
T 2255 0060
sw20.no

T
34 Restaurant 062
34th floor
Radisson SAS Plaza Hotel
Sonja Henies plass 3
T 2205 8000
plaza.oslo.radissonsas.com
Theatercaféen 046
Stortingsgaten 24-26
T 2282 4000
theatercafeen.no
Tiger of Sweden 072
Parkveien 25
T 2336 7710
tigerofsweden.com
Tørst 055
Thorvald Meyers gate 26
T 2287 0467
sult.no
Tronsmo 079
Kristian Augusts gate 19
T 2299 0399
tronsmo.no
Tryvann Vinterpark 088
T 4046 2700
tryvann.no

U
United Bakeries 033
 Frognerveien 58
 T 2411 8728
 unitedbakeries.com
University of Oslo 064
 Karl Johans gate 47

V
Vigeland Sculpture Park 013
 Frongerparken
Viking 072
 vikingfootwear.com
The Villa 040
 Møllergata 23
 thevilla.no
Villa Malla 097
 Stranda 3
 Filtvet, Hurum
 T 3279 5090
 villamalla.no

HOTELS
ADDRESSES AND ROOM RATES

Hotel Bastion 022
Room rates:
double, from NOK 925;
Deluxe Room 316, from NOK 1,400
Skippergaten 7
T 2247 7700
hotelbastion.no

Hotel Continental 029
Room rates:
double, from NOK 1,700;
Deluxe Rooms 507 and 729,
from NOK 2,000
Stortingsgaten 24-26
T 2282 4000
hotel-continental.com

Hotel Folketeateret 016
Room rates:
prices on request
Storgata 21-13
T 2109 6500
www.folketeateret.com

Hotel Gabelshus 020
Room rates:
double, from NOK 1,200;
Room 202, from NOK 1,200;
Rooms 210 and 311, from NOK 1,500;
Suite 501, from NOK 5,000
Gabels gate 16
T 2327 6500
gabelshus.no

Grand Hotel 026
Room rates:
double, from NOK 1,600;
Arctic Room 575, from NOK 2,150;
Ibsen Suite 654, from NOK 6,000
Karl Johans gate 31
T 2321 2000
grand.no

Grims Grenka 017
Room rates:
double, NOK 2,250;
Room 409, NOK 2,250;
Room 202, NOK 2,700;
Room 414, NOK 3,100;
Loft Suite 410, NOK 6,000
Kongens gate 5
T 2310 7200
www.grimsgrenka.no

Juvet Landscape Hotel 101
Room rates:
from NOK 3,500 per person
Alstad
Valldal
T 7025 8652
juvet.com

Lysebu 028
Room rates:
double, from NOK 2,175;
Room 432, from NOK 2,275
Lysebuveien 12
Holmenkollen
T 2151 1000
www.lysebu.com

The Other Side 096
Room rates:
prices on request
Neiden
T 78 996 8203
theotherside.no

Thon Hotel Gyldenløve 016
Room rates:
double, from NOK 1,750
Bogstadveien 20
T 2333 2300
www.thonhotels.com/gyldenlove

Thon Panorama 024
Room rates:
double, from NOK 1,825;
Superior Room 1104, from NOK 2,125;
Rooms 1109 and 1202, from NOK 2,325;
Penthouses 1301 and 1302,
from NOK 15,000
Rådhusgata 7b
T 2331 0800
www.thonhotels.com/oslopanorama

WALLPAPER* CITY GUIDES

Editorial Director
Richard Cook

Art Director
Loran Stosskopf
Editor
Rachael Moloney
Author
Farrid Shamsuddin
Deputy Editor
Jeremy Case
Managing Editor
Jessica Diamond

Chief Designer
Daniel Shrimpton
Designer
Lara Collins
Map Illustrator
Russell Bell

Photography Editor
Sophie Corben
Photography Assistant
Robin Key

Sub-Editors
Stephen Patience
Rachel Ward
Editorial Assistant
Ella Marshall

Interns
Kim Fischer
Lucy Mapstone
Cat Tsang
Kimberly Weireich
Yvette Yarnold

Wallpaper* Group Editor-in-Chief
Tony Chambers
Publishing Director
Gord Ray

Contributors
Marte Frøystad
Hege Golf
Ulf Grønvold
Kristian Berg Harpviken
Sara Henrichs
Helene Aall Henriksen
Bo Mattias Johansson
Ali Hussain Khan
Abeda Khan-Sherwani
Meirion Pritchard
Sondre Sommerfelt
Maren Helly-Hansen Sørbye
Ellie Stathaki

Wallpaper* ® is a registered trademark of IPC Media Limited

All prices are correct at time of going to press, but are subject to change.

PHAIDON

Phaidon Press Limited
Regent's Wharf
All Saints Street
London N1 9PA

Phaidon Press Inc
180 Varick Street
New York, NY 10014

Phaidon® is a registered trademark of Phaidon Press Limited

www.phaidon.com

First published 2009
© 2009 IPC Media Limited

ISBN 978 0 7148 4914 0

A CIP Catalogue record for this book is available from the British Library.

All rights reserved. No part of this publication may be reproduced, stored in a retrieval system or transmitted, in any form or by any means, electronic, mechanical, photocopying, recording or otherwise, without the prior permission of Phaidon Press.

Printed in China

PHOTOGRAPHERS

Per Bernsten
Mortensrud church, pp070-071

Torben Eskerod
Bislett Stadion, pp090-091

Alex Hill
Oslo city view, inside front cover
Operahuset, pp010-011
Gamle Aker church, p012
Vigeland Sculpture Park, p013
Nationaltheatret, pp014-015
Grims Grenka, p017, pp018-019
Hotel Gabelshus, p020, p021
Hotel Bastion, pp022-023
Thon Panorama, p024, p025
Grand Hotel, pp026-027
Lysebu, p028
Hotel Continental, p029, pp030-031
United Bakeries, p033
Grand Café, p035
Südøst, p037
Posthallen, pp038-039
Pascal Café de la Paix, p041
Åpent Bakeri Plaza, p043
Lofoten Fiskerestaurant, p044

Olympen Mat & Vinhus, p045
Theatercaféen, pp046-047
Mauds, p048
Sverre Sætre, p049
Nodee, p050
Bølgen & Moi, p051
Alex Sushi, p052
Hos Thea, p053
Etoile Bar, p054
Sult, p055
No 15, pp056-057
Klosteret, p058
Internasjonalen, p059
La Belle Sole, pp060-061
Julie Ann Seglem, p063
Oslo International School, p065
Ekeberg Restaurant, pp066-067
Rådhuset, p068
Colosseum Kino, p069
Sørensen Østlyngen Møbler, p073
Sjarm, p074
Moods of Norway, p075
Samlersenteret, pp076-077
Secret Society, p078
Damms Antikvariat, p079
Norway Says, pp080-081
Norske Grafikere, p082
Hunting Lodge, p083
Shabby, p084
Passiflora, p085
Freudian Kicks, pp086-087
City Bikes, p089

Barber & Friseursalongen, pp092-093
Artesia Spa, pp094-095

Børre Høstland
National Museum of Architecture, p034

Kristin Saastad
SW20, p042

Timothy Soar
Nobel Peace Center, p036

Øystein Thorvaldsen
Henie Onstad Art Centre, pp098-099

OSLO
A COLOUR-CODED GUIDE TO THE HOT 'HOODS

FROGNER
One of Oslo's most affluent areas comprises impeccable streets of grand, pastel-hued villas

MAJORSTUEN
Established boutiques and gourmet delis create a sophisticated if slightly yuppie vibe

GRÜNERLØKKA
Gentrification has seen the historic squares of this neighbourhood become ever so hip

VIKA
During the week, this is a sober business sector but come Friday it's where the party starts

URANIENBORG AND BRISKEBY
There is a fascinating mix of architectural styles in this charming residential backwater

BISLETT AND ST HANSHAUGEN
A district anchored by St Hanshaugen park draws a young crowd to its laid-back cafés

SENTRUM
There's more here than just chain stores, notably the waterfront view from the Rådhuset

GRØNLAND
Still evolving, Oslo's up-and-coming quarter is currently the most exciting part of the city

For a full description of each neighbourhood, see the Introduction.
Featured venues are colour-coded, according to the district in which they are located.